CH

AMERICAN SPECIAL OPS

THE CIA
The Missions

by Sean McCollum

Consultant:
Ken deGraffenreid
Institute of World Politics
Professor of Intelligence Studies
Washington, D.C.

CAPSTONE PRESS
a capstone imprint

Velocity is published by Capstone Press,
1710 Roe Crest Drive, North Mankato, Minnesota 56003.
www.capstonepub.com

Library of Congress Cataloging-in-Publication Data
McCollum, Sean.
The CIA : the missions / by Sean McCollum.
p. cm.—(Velocity. American special ops)
Includes bibliographical references and index.
Summary: "Describes the CIA, including its history, current missions, and the
    day-to-day activities of CIA workers"—Provided by publisher.
ISBN 978-1-4296-8660-0 (library binding)
ISBN 978-1-4296-9296-0 (ebook PDF)
1. United States. Central Intelligence Agency—Juvenile literature. 2. Intelligence
    service—United States—Juvenile literature. I. Title.
JK468.I6M426 2013
327.1273—dc23   2011053141

Editorial Credits

Carrie Braulick Sheely, editor; Veronica Correia, designer; Laura Manthe,
    production specialist

Photo Credits

AP Images: Chao Soi Cheong, 13 (left), Mikhail Metzel, 5, Staff/Tasnadi, 43 (bottom);
Corbis: Bettmann, 24, 25, Jeffrey L. Rotman, 34 (bottom), Richard A. Bloom, 42,
Roger Ressmeyer, 32-33; Dreamstime: Aleksandar Andjic, 17, Gerry Boughan, 39
(bottom right), Henrik Bolin, 31, Leigh_1, 10 (map); Fotolia: Ben Chams, 21 (bottom
inset); Getty Images: NY Daily News Archive/David Handschuh, 12 (left),
Stegerphoto/Peter Arnold, 45 (inset); Newscom: akg-images, 29 (top), Getty Images/
AFP/DoD, 41, Getty Images/AFP/Saul Loeb, 6 (inset), KRT/Gerald S. Williams, 34
(top), KRT/Keith Myers, 28, RTR/HO, 43 (top), UPI Photo Service, 12 (right), ZUMA
Press, 6-7, 27 (bottom), ZUMA Press/z03, 29 (middle, bottom), 30 (middle);
Shutterstock: andreh, 21 (inset), Andrew Buckin, 38, Axel Wolf, 11 (map), goory, 20
(tv), 21 (tv), Graphic design, cover (hand), iDesign, cover (fingerprint), iofoto, 18-19,
James Steidl, 30 (bottom), jeff gynane, 39 (top right), jokerpro, 44-45 (crowd),
karlovserg, 42, leungchopan, 39 (bottom left), Martin Spurny, 33, Michael Baranski,
14-15, (top), Paul Fleet, 9 (inset), Ralf Kleeman, 35 (inset), Robert F. Balazik, 10
(man), 11 (man), RoxyFer, 39, ruskpp, 8-9, 27 (top), sergign, 44, (tv), 45 (tv),
SVLuma, 30 (top), Tom Mc Nemar, 16, Vasily Smimov, 20 (inset), wtamas, 44 (face);
U. S. Air Force photo by Tech Sgt Sabrina Johnson, 36-37; U. S. Navy photo by
ENCS Lyle G. Becker, 13 (right); U.S. Air Force photo by Master Sgt. Scott Reed,
cover, (UAV), 1, SMSGT Rose Reynolds, 8 (bottom left)

Artistic Effects

Shutterstock

Printed in the United States of America in Stevens Point, Wisconsin.

TABLE of CONTENTS

MISSION ACCOMPLISHED

Thwop ... Thwop ... Thwop ... Thwop ...

On September 26, 2001, a helicopter strained to fly through a mountain pass in Central Asia. On board was a top-secret team of Central Intelligence Agency (CIA) officers. They were slipping into Afghanistan to help overthrow a **radical** group called the Taliban that was controlling the country. Taliban forces were protecting al-Qaida, a terrorist network that had recently struck New York City and Washington, D.C. These attacks had happened two weeks earlier on September 11 and had killed thousands of people.

Step 1

CIA officers handed out millions of dollars to the Northern Alliance to pay for weapons and other supplies.

Step 2

CIA officers and Northern Alliance members set up communications links with trusted U.S. and Afghan commanders. Together, they began planning where, when, and how to attack.

Step 3

The allies mapped the locations of Taliban forces. The CIA officers then joined the Northern Alliance fighters on horseback. They took part in a cavalry charge that overran an important Taliban position.

Step 4

CIA teams guided the arrival of small U.S. special forces units. The two groups worked to direct U.S. jets to bombing targets. More U.S. troops then arrived.

The CIA officers were armed with rifles and handguns. But their most important weapons were between their ears—knowledge and experience. These agents knew the geography and languages of the country. They also knew leaders of Afghanistan who were ready to help them. The officers linked up with a group of Afghan **rebels** called the Northern Alliance who agreed to help.

In the next three months, the CIA and the Northern Alliance took important steps in the war against the Taliban and al-Qaida.

Fact

"Jawbreaker" was the code name given to the CIA officers entering Afghanistan in late September 2001.

Northern Alliance fighters watch Taliban positions on September 26, 2001, in Afghanistan.

Step 5

With the CIA's help, Hamid Karzai returned to Afghanistan. He was an important Afghan political leader who had been forced to leave the country. Karzai eventually became the country's new president.

Step 6

By December 7, the United States and its allies had knocked the Taliban from power. The al-Qaida terrorists no longer had anyone to protect them. The mission known as Operation Jawbreaker was a success. The CIA officers were the first to strike back at al-Qaida and the Taliban.

radical—extreme and often violent
rebel—someone who fights against the government
ally—a person or country working with another for a common cause

WHAT DOES THE CIA DO?

The CIA is part of the United States government. Its headquarters are in Langley, an area in northern Virginia. But it has offices and officers all over the world.

The CIA's most important job is to collect, study, and report **intelligence** about foreign countries. It monitors governments or groups that may be plotting against the United States. It gathers information for use by U.S. government officials, military leaders, and the public. Some CIA operations are very risky, such as Operation Jawbreaker in Afghanistan. Other duties are much less dangerous, although many still require quick thinking, skill, and courage.

CIA headquarters

intelligence—information secretly gathered by spies or electronic devices

The Basic Intelligence Cycle

COLLECTION: CIA officers collect intelligence from around the world.

PLANNING: Decision-makers review the intelligence and decide if action needs to be taken. They may ask CIA officials for additional information.

PROCESSING: CIA officers deliver intelligence to expert analysts for closer review.

ANALYSIS: CIA analysts study the intelligence. They then prepare reports that explain the most important points.

SHARING: The reports are sent to top CIA officials and government decision-makers.

The President's Daily Brief

The Director of National Intelligence (DNI) and the U.S. president oversee the CIA. Each morning the president and vice president receive a top-secret report called the President's Daily Brief (PDB). It contains the latest information about important developments in the world. It also alerts leaders to possible threats to U.S. security. The DNI usually delivers the report, but much of the information in it is supplied by the CIA.

CIA TIMELINE

After World War II (1939–1945), the United States became more involved in international politics and conflicts. The war had expanded the country's roles and responsibilities around the world. U.S. leaders soon realized they needed an organization—the CIA—to help them prepare for the challenges ahead.

1942

The Office of Strategic Services (OSS) is created to collect and analyze military intelligence during World War II. The OSS runs spying operations in Europe, Asia, and elsewhere. It is the forerunner of the CIA.

1947

President Harry S. Truman signs the National Security Act. This law establishes the CIA. The agency's main mission is to keep an eye on the Soviet Union, the main enemy of the United States.

1956

The CIA flies the U-2 spy plane over the Soviet Union for the first time.

2004

A new law creates the office of the Director of National Intelligence. The DNI manages intelligence gathering by the CIA and other agencies.

1986

The CIA forms its Counterterrorism Center to monitor terrorist threats.

1975

Reports surface that the CIA may have planned the overthrow of foreign leaders and conducted illegal spying on American citizens. The agency is put under more government and Congressional oversight.

1960

The CIA launches its first successful spy satellite. It and other early spy satellites are used to take pictures in the Soviet Union to reveal the country's weapons capabilities.

THE CIA AND THE COLD WAR

The United States and the Soviet Union, a **communist** country, were allies during World War II. But after the war, the two competed for power around the world. The Soviets wanted to dominate much of the world. They also wanted to block the spread of U.S. military and economic power. The United States wanted to protect freedom and stop the spread of communism. This competition became known as the Cold War. Both sides built huge militaries of soldiers and weapons. They aimed nuclear missiles at each other. The CIA used spies, spy planes, and spy satellites to monitor Soviet activities. At the same time, Soviet government and military agencies tried to uncover American secrets. These Soviet agencies were known by the initials KGB and GRU. The Cold War ended when the Soviet Union broke apart in 1991.

United States

☆ **Bay of Pigs (1961):** In 1959 communist rebels took over Cuba. It became a Soviet ally. CIA-trained Cuban rebels planned to overthrow the communists there. But the rebels were outgunned as they came ashore at the Bay of Pigs. U.S. President John F. Kennedy refused to provide U.S. military help. The attempted invasion was an embarrassing CIA failure.

Soviet Union

⭐ **Atomic Spies (1940s and 1950s):** Soviet agents recruited U.S. and British scientists to steal U.S. secrets about dangerous atomic weapons.

⭐ **U-2 Incident (1960):** The Soviets shot down a CIA U-2 spy plane. The event threatened the CIA's program that used high-flying jets to photograph Soviet sites.

⭐ **Oleg Penkovsky (1961-1963):** Oleg Penkovsky, a Soviet missile expert, passed important secrets to American and British spies. He was caught in 1962 and killed by the Soviet government.

⭐ **Vietnam War (1959-1975):** Soviet agents supplied North Vietnamese forces with intelligence and weapons. The North Vietnamese were fighting the South Vietnamese, U.S. forces, and their allies.

⭐ **Cuban Missile Crisis (1962):** The Soviets began installing nuclear missiles in Cuba. They wanted to help prevent a U.S. invasion of Cuba and gain a strategic advantage. But soon a CIA spy plane photographed the missile sites. The two sides stood on the brink of nuclear war until a deal was made and the missiles were removed.

⭐ **Afghanistan Invasion (1979-1989):** The Soviets invaded Afghanistan in 1979. In response, the CIA supplied Afghan fighters with weapons and intelligence to drive out the Soviets.

communist—relating to communism, a political and economic system where freedom is restricted and the government owns almost all businesses and property

recruit—to try to convince someone to help or join an organization

THE CIA TAKES ON TERRORISM

After the Cold War, a different issue grabbed headlines—global terrorism. At first the CIA struggled to understand and stop this new threat. The Soviet Union had been the CIA's focus for many years. The agency didn't have enough agents in place to spy on terrorist groups based in the Middle East and Afghanistan. Terrorist groups, especially al-Qaida, took advantage of this weakness.

BOMBING OF THE WORLD TRADE CENTER (1993)

Terrorists used a van filled with explosives to attack New York's World Trade Center. The blast killed six people. The terrorists were a group of Islamic extremists. They were later caught, tried, and imprisoned.

U.S. EMBASSY BOMBINGS (1998)

Truck bombs exploded outside U.S. embassies in the African countries of Kenya and Tanzania. The blasts killed more than 200 people. CIA officers investigated. Al-Qaida was suspected of carrying out the attack.

ATTACK ON THE U.S.S. *COLE* (2000)

Al-Qaida terrorists rammed a bomb-packed speedboat into the side of the U.S.S. *Cole* while the ship was docked in Yemen. The blast blew a big hole in the side of the U.S. destroyer and killed 17 American sailors.

9/11 (2001)

Al-Qaida terrorists hijacked four passenger jets in the United States. The terrorists crashed two jets into the Twin Towers of the World Trade Center. Another plane was flown into the Pentagon, the headquarters of the U.S. military in Washington, D.C. The fourth plane crashed in a Pennsylvania field. Some people think it may have been headed for the White House. Almost 3,000 people were killed in the attacks.

The CIA and other U.S. intelligence agencies were criticized for not having done enough to prevent these attacks. But after 9/11, the CIA focused on destroying al-Qaida and other terrorist groups.

embassy—the official place in a foreign country where a government official called an ambassador lives and works

ONGOING CIA MISSIONS

The CIA monitors ongoing threats around the world. The agency works with local spies and intelligence organizations in foreign countries. Together the groups find and stop people from plotting to harm the United States and U.S. overseas interests.

DRUG RINGS: Many illegal drugs in the United States come from drug operations in Asia and Latin America. The CIA cooperates with foreign and U.S. law enforcement agencies to try to break up these drug rings.

GLOBAL TERRORISM: Since 2001 the CIA has worked to break up terrorist networks in the Middle East, Central Asia, and Africa. Many al-Qaida leaders have been caught. But terrorists continue to find ways to attack people and places in the United States and elsewhere. The CIA tries to stop them in a variety of ways. These methods include using spies, surveillance equipment, and unmanned aerial vehicles (UAVs).

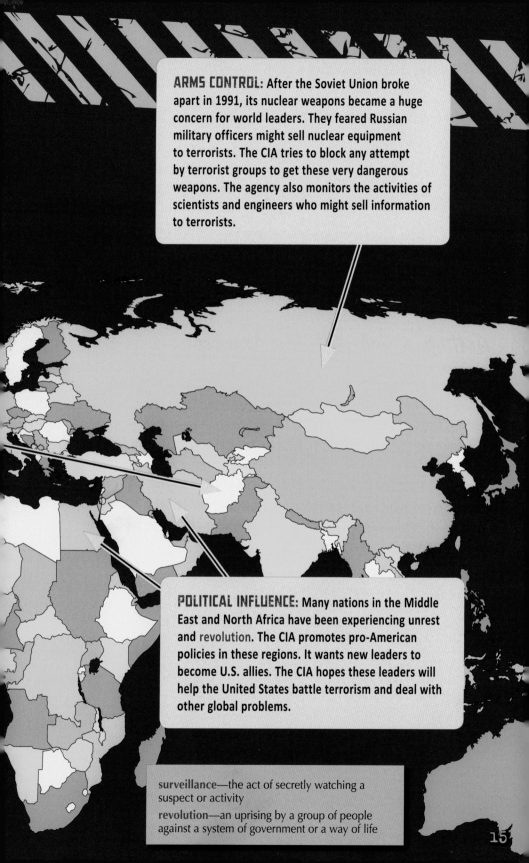

ARMS CONTROL: After the Soviet Union broke apart in 1991, its nuclear weapons became a huge concern for world leaders. They feared Russian military officers might sell nuclear equipment to terrorists. The CIA tries to block any attempt by terrorist groups to get these very dangerous weapons. The agency also monitors the activities of scientists and engineers who might sell information to terrorists.

POLITICAL INFLUENCE: Many nations in the Middle East and North Africa have been experiencing unrest and revolution. The CIA promotes pro-American policies in these regions. It wants new leaders to become U.S. allies. The CIA hopes these leaders will help the United States battle terrorism and deal with other global problems.

surveillance—the act of secretly watching a suspect or activity

revolution—an uprising by a group of people against a system of government or a way of life

CIA JOBS:
TRAINING AND DUTIES

Only a small percentage of CIA workers are spies. The CIA calls its spies operations officers. These employees work in secret gathering information. But most other CIA workers are language specialists, computer experts, lawyers, economists, and other professionals.

Getting a Job With the Agency

Getting a job with the CIA is a big challenge. All CIA workers must be U.S. citizens and almost all are college graduates. Some people are secretly approached because of their language abilities, computer skills, or other talents. Intelligence specialists in the U.S. Army, Navy, or Air Force are sometimes recruited. But others can apply for jobs too. The CIA does deep background checks on all applicants. It investigates a candidate's family, friends, and habits to help ensure that applicants can be trusted. Applicants must also pass a lie detector test.

CIA JOB OPPORTUNITIES IN:

- Analysis
- Clandestine Service
- Language
- Science and Engineering
- Information Technology
- Security

Training

If accepted, CIA candidates go through the agency's one-year professional training program. They are taught many different skills and tested on them. These skills may include foreign languages, surveillance, and self-defense. Candidates for secret, or clandestine, service jobs receive an additional year of in-depth training.

lie detector test being performed

Fact

"The Farm" in Virginia and Harvey Point on the coast of North Carolina are said to be two of the CIA's top-secret training facilities.

THE NATIONAL CLANDESTINE SERVICE

The CIA's National Clandestine Service (NCS) oversees the CIA's operations officers. These officers seek and find pieces of information. Then CIA analysts put the pieces together.

Cover

Some CIA operations officers serve under "official cover" at U.S. embassies. These positions give them diplomatic protection. If they are caught spying, they can be thrown out of the country but not jailed. Other CIA officers work under "nonofficial cover." They spy while pretending to work other jobs overseas. These jobs often give them reasons to travel and meet many people. If an officer with nonofficial cover is caught, the U.S. government and CIA may deny any connection to him or her.

Developing Assets

A main mission of CIA officers is to develop assets. Assets are people inside a government, business, or organization who can help get information for the CIA. CIA officers look for people in important positions who might have reasons to help the United States. An operations officer will often offer money or some other benefit in exchange for a person's help. But CIA officers must be careful about who they recruit. An asset may be a **double agent**. A double agent often feeds misleading information to operations officers to trick them.

Fact

Information from people is known as "human intelligence." In the CIA this word is often shortened to HUMINT.

cover—a role or career used to disguise a spy's real job
double agent—a person who appears to help or work for one country's spy agency but who is really loyal to another

ANALYSTS:
THE BRAINS
IN THE BACKGROUND

Analysts work to put the big intelligence puzzle together. They review intelligence reports from the field. They study information that might fill in details of their investigation. They review foreign news stories, intercepted e-mails, and spy satellite images. They also try to foresee what might happen next.

Counterterrorism Analysts

Counterterrorism analysts study terrorist groups to understand what they may be planning. If there are signs that an attack is looming, analysts alert top CIA and military officials. They may then help form a plan to stop the attack.

Economic and Political Analysts

What is changing in the world right now? How will it affect the United States? These are the questions CIA economic and political analysts constantly ask. They want to figure out if a country is on the brink of an economic crisis. They look for clues that a government is ripe for a revolution. U.S. leaders then use this knowledge to prepare for what might happen.

Science and Technology Analysts

Imagine that a country boasts it has deadly chemical weapons. Is that government telling the truth? Or is it bluffing to make its enemies nervous? The CIA's science and technology analysts would uncover the facts. Accurate science and technology intelligence helps U.S. leaders avoid wars and prepare for them.

intercept—to catch and stop the progress of something

WOULD YOU HAVE WHAT IT TAKES?

The CIA has many jobs that can fit a wide variety of personalities and skill sets. For example, officers in the National Clandestine Service must be quick-thinkers and remain cool under pressure. Analysts must be able to piece together many details and separate facts from rumors. Technical experts must be genius engineers to create gadgets for important missions.

Do you think you might like to work with the CIA some day? This chart can help you explore what the CIA looks for in its employees. Match the color coding in each text block to the career groups at the bottom.

I like taking tough classes at school and push myself hard in sports and other activities.

Most CIA workers like to challenge themselves.

I enjoy trying to solve complex puzzles.

CIA analysts have to sort through tons of data to figure out the big picture.

I enjoy learning about other cultures.

I think telling stories and acting in plays is a lot of fun.

I like writing reports.

The abilities to play different roles and win the trust of others are key skills for CIA operations officers.

No matter their position, CIA workers must be able to explain situations clearly in reports. This skill is especially important for analysts.

Understanding other cultures helps CIA officers work with people from different countries. It also helps analysts choose the best course of action.

I enjoy working with others to solve problems.

Good teamwork can mean the difference between a mission's success or failure.

I consider myself a risk-taker.

Operations officers must be very brave. Their lives are on the line if they are caught spying.

I enjoy studying other languages.

The ability to speak and understand different languages helps CIA workers in many positions.

I rarely get nervous when I'm taking a tough test at school, even if I don't know all the answers.

Keeping a clear head under pressure is very important for CIA officers.

If people have a problem with their computer or cell phone, they always come to me for help.

The CIA relies on IT experts to keep its computers and technological devices running smoothly. These experts also help keep sensitive information on computers secure.

I think it is important to know what is going on in politics and world affairs.

CIA officers must be knowledgeable about what is going on in the world.

I am good at building and fixing gadgets. I like to take apart devices to see how they work.

The CIA needs skilled engineers and scientists to make high-tech gear that spies use.

I enjoy exercising and staying fit.

CIA officers in the field need to have good physical fitness to deal with potentially dangerous situations.

Intelligence Analysis

Business, Information Technology, and Security

Clandestine Service

Science, Engineering, and Technology

The SPECIAL ACTIVITIES DIVISION

Sometimes the CIA does more than gather intelligence. It takes action. The CIA's Special Activities Division carries out many of these top-secret missions. Two main groups make up this division. The Special Operations Group (SOG) conducts **paramilitary** operations. The Political Action Group works in secret to help change a country's political situation.

Unclassified:

Poland's Solidarity Movement

In 1980 members of the workers' union Solidarity went on strike in Poland. They were speaking out against Poland's communist government. The CIA's Political Action Group secretly supplied money, a printing press, and even TV broadcasting gear to Solidarity. The group used the support to organize large protests. Communist leaders were finally forced to give in to some of Solidarity's demands. The Solidarity movement helped lead to free elections in Poland and the end of communist rule there in 1989.

Solidarity leader Lech Walesa speaks to a crowd of supporters in 1980.

The Risk of Blowback

When the CIA takes action, there is always a risk the consequences will "blowback" to affect the United States. CIA involvement in Iran in the 1950s is an example of a situation that caused blowback. In 1953 the Political Action Group helped overthrow Iran's popular president, Mohammad Mosaddeq. The United States was upset that Mosaddeq had grabbed control of Iran's oil industry from a British company. The United States helped replace him with Mohammad Reza Shah Pahlavi. Pahlavi crushed all political opponents.

In 1979 Pahlavi was overthrown during the Iranian Revolution. Many Iranians hated the United States for supporting Pahlavi and interfering with their country. The revolutionaries overran the U.S. Embassy in Tehran and took 66 Americans hostage. Fourteen were soon released, but 52 hostages were held for more than a year. Iran and U.S. relations remain icy even today.

After Iranians took control of the U.S. Embassy, they burned several U.S. flags on top of the building.

paramilitary—a military force that is not part of a government-run army

SPECIAL

OPERATIONS

GROUP

The CIA's Special Operations Group conducts paramilitary operations and combat missions. Members of the group do not wear uniforms, so they cannot be identified. They often cooperate with branches of the U.S. military. However, they are not under military command. This fact makes them different from special operations groups such as the Navy SEALs and Army Rangers.

SOG Officers

Almost all SOG officers start their careers in U.S. military branches. They are recruited because of their proven skill at carrying out dangerous combat missions. If the United States plans a military attack, SOG units are often the first Americans to go in. They operate behind enemy lines, conducting sabotage, spying, and scouting missions. Sometimes SOG units train and organize local fighters.

sabotage—damage or destruction of property that is done on purpose

The Memorial Wall

More than 100 small stars are carved in a wall in the entryway of the CIA headquarters building. Each star represents a CIA officer killed in the line of duty. Most mark the sacrifice of SOG officers. Beneath the stars rests the "Book of Honor." It lists the names of those who have died. But about 50 names have been left blank. Their identities are kept secret to protect their friends, family, and fellow CIA officers.

IN HONOR OF THOSE MEMBERS
OF THE CENTRAL INTELLIGENCE AGENCY
WHO GAVE THEIR LIVES IN THE SERVICE OF THEIR COUNTRY

Chapter 4

TOOLS AND TACTICS OF CIA SPIES

Spying usually includes two main steps: gathering secret information and passing the information to others for analysis. The CIA teaches its spies how to use a variety of methods and tools to succeed in their shadowy missions. Throughout the CIA's history, a variety of spying devices have been invented and used. Here are just a few:

Corona Spy Satellite

The Corona spy satellite was developed to photograph the Soviet Union, China, and other countries from space. Its first successful launch took place in 1960. Corona ejected the film in a special capsule. A special plane flew out to catch the capsule.

Pinhole Cameras

The CIA and other intelligence agencies invented very small cameras called pinhole cameras. They are so small that they can be disguised as matchboxes, lighters, pens, and watches. They can also be hidden inside clocks, smoke detectors, and other common items.

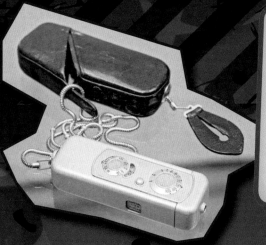

Minox Camera

German-Latvian inventor Walter Zapp invented the Minox miniature camera in the 1920s. Smaller than a candy bar, it was easy to use and easy to hide. It became a favorite tool of spies from many countries.

"Bellybuster" Hand-crank Audio Drill

The "bellybuster" drill was used to drill holes into walls for hiding electronic listening devices called bugs. The drill's base was held against the stomach, giving the device its nickname. The bellybuster was used in the 1950s and 1960s.

The Wizards of Langley

The CIA's Directorate of Science and Technology (DS&T) makes high-tech gear for operations officers. The scientists and engineers are so good at their craft they have been nicknamed "The Wizards of Langley." Their gadgets have included everything from tracking and listening devices to cameras and spy satellites. One of the group's first projects was developing a lithium-iodine battery.

The DS&T shared this battery's technology with the public in the early 1960s. Today lithium-iodine batteries are used in medical devices such as heart pacemakers.

lithium-iodine battery

OLD TRICKS OF THE SPY TRADE

THE BRUSH PASS

Two agents bump into each other in a train station. They quickly exchange the newspapers they are carrying—newspapers that contain coded messages. They then walk away from each other as if nothing happened.

DEAD DROPS

Would you pick up a dead rat? Probably not! And that's why spies have used freeze-dried rat bodies as dead drops. A dead drop is a container or location for secretly passing information between people. It is usually disguised as an easily ignored object, like a rock or a stump. The contents are inserted. Then the sender alerts the receiver to make the pick-up.

SECRET SIGNALS

To signal they want a meeting, spies may leave a secret sign in a public place. CIA traitor Aldrich Ames would draw a chalk line on a big blue U.S. mailbox. The mark alerted Soviet agents that he had left information at a dead drop.

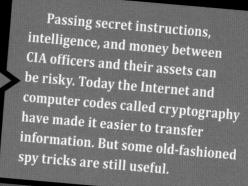

Passing secret instructions, intelligence, and money between CIA officers and their assets can be risky. Today the Internet and computer codes called cryptography have made it easier to transfer information. But some old-fashioned spy tricks are still useful.

Surveillance Detection

During a mission, CIA operations officers walk or drive around before a meeting. They are watching for clues that they are being followed. If a car or pedestrian seems to be tailing them, spies abandon the mission.

CIA CASE STUDY:
Adolf Tolkachev

In January 1977, a CIA officer based in Moscow, Russia, stopped for gas. A Russian man walked up and put a note on the front seat of the American's car. The note said he wanted to speak to an American official. The Russian's name was Adolf Tolkachev, and he became one of the CIA's most valuable spies.

Helping the CIA

Tolkachev was an electronics engineer who worked on military radar systems. He had important information about Soviet weapons that he wanted to pass to the United States.

Risky Business

To communicate, the CIA and Tolkachev used many methods, including secret signals. Tolkachev would ask for a meeting by parking his car in a certain place facing in a certain direction. His CIA officer used an old dirty mitten as a dead drop. Inside, he hid miniature cameras for Tolkachev to photograph secret documents. Tolkachev also used secret writing to communicate with his CIA officer. He gave the CIA a great deal of valuable information, and the CIA paid him well.

One of the Soviet planes Tolkachev supplied information about to the CIA was the MiG-29.

Tolkachev worked near the U.S. Embassy in Moscow. The closeness of the two locations made it easier for Tolkachev to contact an embassy worker without looking suspicious.

A Deadly End

In 1985 Tolkachev's CIA contact was caught while going to a meeting with Tolkachev. A CIA **mole** had told the Soviets about the operation. The CIA officer who worked with Tolkachev was thrown out of the country. Tolkachev was not so lucky. The mole had betrayed him too. He was arrested and killed.

mole—a spy who works within the government of a country in order to supply secret information to another country

SURVEILLANCE TOOLS, CAMERAS, AND BUGS

With the arrival of the digital age, electronic gadgets have become smaller and more powerful. The CIA has used these leaps in technology to improve its spying capabilities.

Cameras

Tiny cameras can be hidden in clocks, smoke detectors, baseball caps, sunglasses—even fake buttons and fake screws. In the past, these pictures had to be developed using special chemicals. Now digital images can be sent instantly using phones or other high-tech devices.

Bugs

These listening devices allow CIA officers to overhear secret plans. Most bugs have three parts—a microphone, battery, and transmitter. The transmitter sends the signal to a listening station. Bugs can be installed in phones or hidden in rooms. One device called a laser monitoring system can simply be pointed at a window from outside. It senses the sound vibrations from inside, allowing the listener to hear the conversation.

Computer Surveillance

A computer keystroke recording program can track the keystrokes of a computer user. What the person types can then be decoded later.

Counter-Surveillance

CIA operations officers must be aware that they could be under surveillance themselves. To guard against being monitored, the officers use devices such as signal detectors. These detectors scan for signals from hidden microphones or video cameras.

Fact

In the mid-1960s, the CIA implanted a microphone and battery in a cat's body. An antenna was placed in the cat's tail. But the project, called "Acoustic Kitty," was never used successfully.

EYES IN THE SKY

Predator UAV

SATELLITE ANTENNA: The satellite antenna is inside the UAV's nose. The pilot commands the UAV using satellites when there is no direct link available.

NOSE CAMERA: This camera broadcasts color images to help the pilot control the UAV by remote control.

VARIABLE APERTURE CAMERAS: These are the UAV's main eyes for spying. One of these cameras is infrared. The infrared camera allows the Predator to see in the dark.

LENGTH: 27 feet (8.2 meters)

Fact

The CIA is developing mini-UAVs that will be able to fly unnoticed into enemy territory.

CIA surveillance includes keeping an eye on enemies from the sky. Photographs can reveal another country's military secrets. The CIA used satellites to monitor the Soviet Union's nuclear missiles and military movements during the Cold War. Today spy satellites can zoom in on any place in the world. In combat zones, unmanned aerial vehicles can keep track of enemy movements and beam images back to CIA analysts.

BODY: The body of the Predator is a mixture of carbon and quartz fibers blended with a strong material called Kevlar.

MISSILES: The Predator can carry missiles to attack targets.

SYNTHETIC APERTURE RADAR PROCESSOR: This device can find targets through clouds or smoke. It works with an antenna in the front of the UAV.

WINGSPAN: 48.7 feet (14.8 meters)
* Wingspan is measured from one wing tip to the other.

HEIGHT:
6.9 feet
(2.1 meters)

CYBER SPIES

Information technology (IT) and the Internet have changed how the world works. The CIA has top computer security specialists to help deal with rapidly changing technology. These specialists use the Internet to spy on computer networks of other countries. They also block cyber attacks against the U.S. government and its computer systems.

Computer Analysis and Communication

CIA analysts rely a great deal on IT and computer software. Computers sort through huge amounts of information and pick out useful details. CIA operations officers and their assets communicate through the Internet using encryption. This communication method saves them the trouble—and danger—of meeting face-to-face.

HOW ENCRYPTION WORKS

message:
Deliver documents to dead drop XYZ at 1:00 a.m.

encrypted message:
fdsak jksd8n XYnkela snkde skj fjdk93 397u3k

message:
Deliver documents to dead drop XYZ at 1:00 a.m.

encryption key

decryption key

Cyber Attacks

The good news is that computers help a fast-paced world run more smoothly. The bad news is that a cyber attack on a computer network can be very destructive. Hackers can steal secrets or damage IT systems. Security experts worry that someday a cyber attack could shut down electrical systems for large regions of the United States. Hackers might even affect U.S. military systems by shutting down high-tech weapons. Preventing such attacks has been added to the CIA's responsibilities.

POSSIBLE HACKER TARGETS

communications systems

transportation systems

power and utility companies

banking and financial institutions

information technology—the use of computers and other electronic equipment to find, create, store, or communicate information

cyber attack—an attack that uses the Internet to damage or take control of a computer network

hacker—a person who is an expert at getting into a computer system illegally

Chapter 5

TRIUMPHS AND CHALLENGES

Around the clock and around the world, CIA members work and fight in the shadows. Because of the need for secrecy, many CIA successes will never be known. But here are a few that the world has learned about.

OPERATION IVY BELLS (1971):

For this operation, the CIA worked with the U.S. Navy and the National Security Agency (NSA). A submarine and deep-sea divers were sent to put a wiretap on an undersea communications cable used by the Soviet military. They were able to collect valuable information about Soviet naval operations.

PROJECT AZORIAN (1974):

In 1968 a Soviet submarine sank in the Pacific Ocean. The CIA wanted to retrieve the wreck and any secrets it contained. In 1974 a specially built ship raised part of the sub, including two nuclear-tipped torpedoes. The mission gave the United States a better understanding of the Soviet Union's nuclear weapons.

FINDING BIN LADEN (2011):

Osama bin Laden was the leader of the al-Qaida terrorist organization. He helped plan the 9/11 attacks and other terrorist attacks against U.S. targets. The CIA hunted him for more than 10 years. In 2010 the CIA connected clues that hinted he was hiding in a guarded building in Pakistan. CIA officers sneaked into position and put the compound under surveillance from a nearby house. They gathered enough intelligence to determine bin Laden was likely there. On May 1, 2011, U.S. special forces attacked the hideout. Bin Laden was killed.

BIN LADEN'S COMPOUND

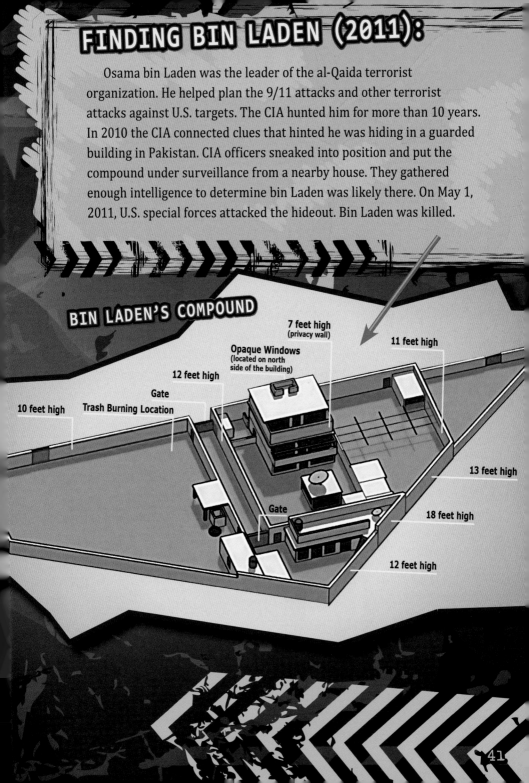

7 feet high
(privacy wall)

Opaque Windows
(located on north side of the building)

11 feet high

12 feet high

Gate

Trash Burning Location

10 feet high

13 feet high

Gate

18 feet high

12 feet high

CIA MOLES AND TRAITORS

Intelligence officers from other countries sometimes recruit CIA officers and turn them into moles. These traitors continue to work for the CIA but steal top-secret information and pass it to foreign agents. Why do they do it? Usually for money.

ALDRICH AMES

Aldrich Ames served as a CIA analyst and counterintelligence officer. His main job was to search for people spying against the CIA. Ironically, he became the kind of traitor he was supposed to catch. Ames was having money troubles in the early 1980s. He contacted Soviet officials and offered to sell them secrets. The Soviets agreed. Ames handed over the identities of many CIA assets. Some of these people in the Soviet Union were captured and killed. Ames received $4.6 million in return for this information. The CIA eventually grew suspicious, and Ames was arrested in 1993. He is considered the most destructive mole in CIA history. Ames is serving a life sentence in prison.

Harold James Nicholson worked as a CIA officer from 1980 to 1996. He collected intelligence about the Soviet Union and managed CIA spy networks overseas. He even served as an instructor of CIA trainees. In the early 1990s, Russian intelligence officers approached Nicholson and asked him to spy for them. In return for $300,000, he sold top-secret photos, computer files, and the names of pro-American spies stationed in Russia. He was arrested in 1996 and sent to prison.

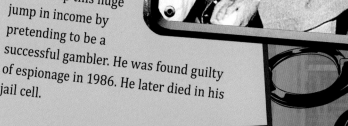

Larry Wu-Tai Chin was a Chinese language translator for the CIA and a double agent for China. He may have earned as much as $1 million by selling CIA secrets. He covered up this huge jump in income by pretending to be a successful gambler. He was found guilty of espionage in 1986. He later died in his jail cell.

The CIA never stops finding new ways to carry out its missions. In fact, the CIA of tomorrow may already be here—and we just don't know it yet.

Facial Recognition Software

Security cameras scan city streets every minute of every day. A computer zooms in on a face and matches it to a suspected terrorist. The computer alerts a CIA officer who moves in and puts the suspect under surveillance. Sound unreal? Tools with these capabilities are already being developed.

Text message intercept:
Meet me at ...
sent to: 555-808-1111

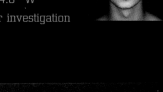

Name: Napoleon Xerxes
Date of birth: 06 May 1992
Latitude: 44.2° N,
Longitude: 94.0° W
Status: under investigation

Monitoring Calls and the Internet

Around the world, billions of phone calls are made every day. Intelligence agencies are developing powerful software programs that scan these calls. They try to match the voices on the calls to recorded voiceprints of suspects. They also study call patterns and intercept and monitor calls and text messages.

Other programs study Internet activities. These programs search for messages and patterns that may help the CIA uncover criminal or terrorist activity.

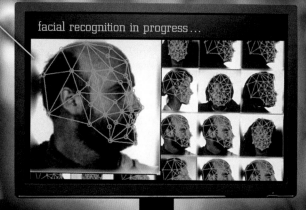

facial recognition in progress...

Fact

In 2011 the CIA used facial recognition software to help confirm that Osama bin Laden had been killed in the raid on his compound.

GLOSSARY

ally (AL-eye)—a person or country united with another for a common cause

communist (KAHM-yuh-nist)—relating to communism, a way of organizing a country so that all the land, houses, and factories belong to the government

cover (KUH-ver)—a role or career used to disguise a spy's real job

cyber attack (SYE-bur uh-TAK)—an attack that uses the Internet to damage or take control of a computer network

double agent (DUH-buhl AY-juhnt)—a person who appears to help or work for one country's spy agency but who is really loyal to another

embassy (EM-buh-see)—the official place in a foreign country where a government official called an ambassador lives and works

hacker (HAK-ur)—a person who is an expert at getting into a computer system illegally

information technology (in-fur-MAY-shuhn tek-NOL-uh-jee)—the use of computers and other electronic equipment to find, create, store, or communicate information

intelligence (in-TEL-uh-jenss)—information secretly gathered by spies

intercept (in-tur-SEPT)—to catch and stop the progress of something

mole (MOHL)—a spy who works within the government of a country in order to supply secret information to another country

paramilitary (pa-ruh-MIL-uh-ter-ee)—a military force that is not part of an official army

radical (RAD-i-kuhl)—extreme and often violent

rebel (REB-uhl)—someone who fights against the government

recruit (ri-KROOT)—to try to convince someone to help or join an organization

revolution (rev-uh-LOO-shun)—an uprising against a government or a way of life

sabotage (SAB-uh-tahzh)—damage of property that is done on purpose

surveillance (suhr-VAY-luhnss)—the act of secretly watching a suspect or activity

READ MORE

Burgan, Michael. *Spies and Traitors: Stories of Masters of Deception.* Bad Guys. Mankato, Minn.: Capstone Press, 2010.

Platt, Richard. *Spy.* DK Eyewitness Books. New York: DK Publishing, 2009.

Streissguth, Thomas. *The Security Agencies of the United States: How the CIA, FBI, NSA and Homeland Security Keep Us Safe.* Berkeley Heights, N.J.: Enslow Publishers, 2012.

INTERNET SITES

FactHound offers a safe, fun way to find Internet sites related to this book. All of the sites on FactHound have been researched by our staff.

Here's all you do:

Visit *www.facthound.com*

Type in this code: 9781429686600

INDEX